Parts of the body

Furniture

Fruit

Opposites

Jobs

Special days

Vegetables

Animals

Food and drinks

Vehicles

Mein erstes
BILDWÖRTERBUCH
ENGLISCH

von Ute Müller-Wolfangel
und Cornelia Pardall
mit Bildern von Barbara Scholz

FISCHER Duden Kinderbuch

MIX
Papier aus verantwor-
tungsvollen Quellen
FSC® C012536

3. Auflage 2016

Erschienen bei FISCHER Duden Kinderbuch

© 2013 S. Fischer Verlag GmbH,
Hedderichstr. 114, D-60596 Frankfurt am Main
„Duden" ist eine eingetragene Marke
des Verlags Bibliographisches Institut GmbH, Berlin.

Layout und Satz: Michelle Vollmer, Mainz
Umschlagkonzept: Sabine Reddig

Druck und Bindung: Theiss GmbH, St. Stefan im Lavanthal
Printed in Austria
ISBN 978-3-7373-3046-6

Inhalt

Liebe Eltern, liebe Lehrerinnen und Lehrer,

Computer, T-Shirt, Skateboard – diese englischen Wörter kennen Kinder aus ihrer unmittelbaren Lebenswelt und benutzen sie ganz selbstverständlich in ihrer täglichen Sprache. An dieses unbefangene Umgehen mit Wörtern aus einer Fremdsprache knüpft „Mein erstes Bildwörterbuch Englisch" an.

Der erste Teil ist in **21 Themengebiete aus dem Erlebnis- und Erfahrungshorizont** von Kindern eingeteilt. Alle Begriffe werden in Bild und Wort dargestellt. Jedem Thema sind passende Sprachmuster, „First phrases", beigefügt, in die gelernte Wörter der jeweiligen Seite eingesetzt werden können. Am Ende des ersten Teils sind alle „First phrases" mit ihrer deutschen Übersetzung aufgelistet.

Im zweiten Teil steht der **aktive Umgang mit der englischen Sprache** in Form von Spielen, Liedern und Bildergeschichten im Mittelpunkt. Die zu den Bildergeschichten gehörigen „First phrases" unterstützen die Verständigung auf Englisch in Alltagssituationen. Im Anschluss sind diese „First phrases" ins Deutsche übersetzt.

Der dritte Teil dieses Buches ist ein **kleines Wörterbuch** zum Nachschlagen. Dort sind alle englischen Wörter des ersten Teils mit Lautschrift alphabetisch geordnet und ins Deutsche übersetzt. Auf der letzten Seite ist eine Lautschrifttabelle abgebildet.

Die **Audio-CD** enthält alle Wörter des ersten und zweiten Teils von Muttersprachlern gesprochen. So werden die Kinder mit der richtigen Aussprache vertraut. Die Wörter der Themenseiten sind jeweils mit ihrer deutschen Übersetzung zu hören. Anschließend wird jedes Wort in das dazugehörige Sprachmuster eingesetzt. Durch die Wiederholung prägen sich die Wörter besonders gut ein. Die kleinen CD-Symbole auf jeder Seite geben die Nummer des Tracks an, unter dem der entsprechende Inhalt auf der Aufnahme zu finden ist.

Viel Freude beim Englischlernen!

Die Autorinnen

Das ist Nessie, die Leitfigur dieses Buches.
Sie ist schon ein Englischprofi
und stellt die Themen vor.

Vorschläge zur Nutzung dieses Buches

Teil 1

1. Wörter
Sprechen Sie das englische Wort vor und deuten Sie auf das dazugehörige Bild. Lassen Sie dann das Kind das Wort mehrmals nachsprechen, wobei es ebenfalls auf das Bild zeigt.

2. Sprachmuster
Sprechen Sie den vorgegebenen Satz vor und lassen Sie ihn
dann vom Kind nachsprechen. Ersetzen Sie anschließend die bildlich
dargestellten Wörter durch andere Begriffe von der Seite.

Teil 2

1. Lieder und Reime
Singen oder sprechen Sie einen Vers vor und wiederholen Sie ihn mit
dem Kind gemeinsam.

2. Bildergeschichten
Sprechen Sie die Dialoge einzeln vor und lassen Sie sie dann vom
Kind nachsprechen. Wenden Sie die „First phrases" auch in eigenen
kleinen Spielsituationen an.

Alternativ können die Wörter, Sätze und Verse von der CD abgehört
werden. Geübte Kinder nutzen dieses Angebot sicher bald auch
selbstständig.

Buggy

Jeans

Clown

Sweatshirt

Cornflakes

Muffins

Chips

Nessie

Milk-shake

Teddy

Mountain-bike

Gameboy

Inline-skates

Discman

6

Animals

dolphin

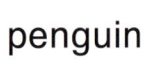

penguin

lion

elephant

monkey

bear

tiger

giraffe

sheep

hen

duck

goat

goose

cow

pig

horse

The  lives in the zoo.

The lives on the farm.

Pets

guinea pig

bird

mouse

puppy

dog

hamster

rabbit

kitten

cat

parrot

goldfish

turtle

First phrases

5 Where is the  ?

Here it is.

11

Toys

teddy bear

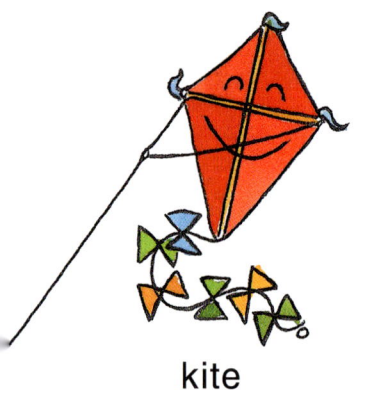

kite

football

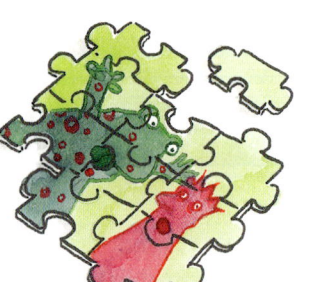

jigsaw puzzle

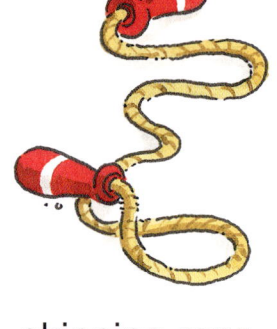

skipping rope

building bricks

train set

toy car

play dough

doll

ball

puppets

ghost

witch

cowboy   princess

king

7 Can I have the  , please?

Here you are.

Yes, you can. / No, you can't.

13

Food and drinks

egg

bread

butter

cheese

lemonade

pepper

salt

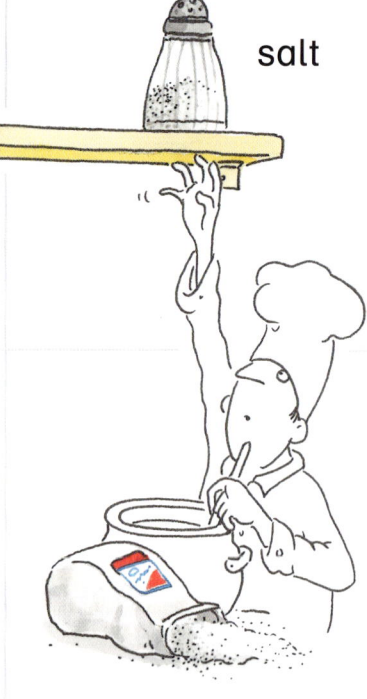

juice

mineral water

sugar

ham

sausage

jam

honey

hot chocolate

milk

tea

Pass the , please.

Here it is.

Fruit

pineapple

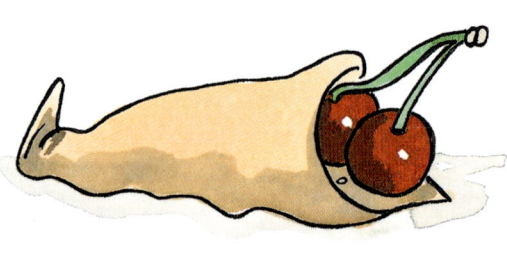

cherries

strawberries

grapes

orange

watermelon

apple

16

pear

banana

kiwi fruit

plum

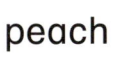

peach

lemon

Can I have a , please?

Can I have some 🍒, please?

Yes, you can. / No, you can't.

Vegetables

potato

cabbage

red pepper

beans

radish

onion

cucumber

carrot

lettuce

tomato

mushroom

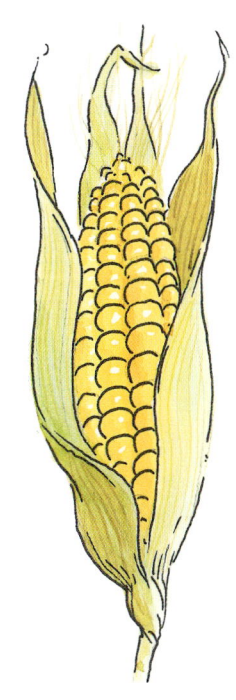

corn

cauliflower

peas

13 I like eating .

I don't like eating .

Parts of the body

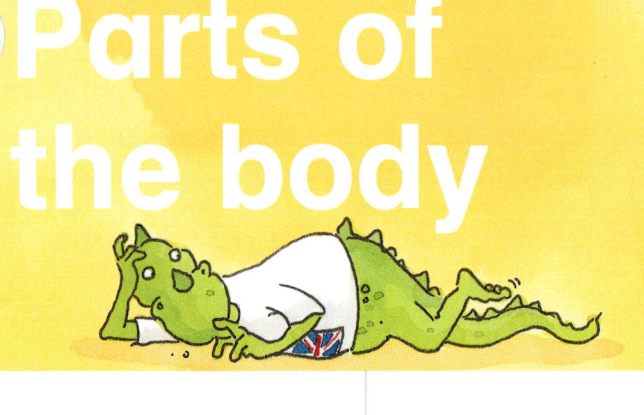

head

hair

ear

face

mouth

nose

chin

eye

tooth

tongue

neck

finger

hand

shoulder

arm

elbow

body

toe

knee

leg

foot

15 Show me your !

This is my .

Family

child/children

parents

father

mother

daughter

son

baby

grandparents

grandfather

grandmother

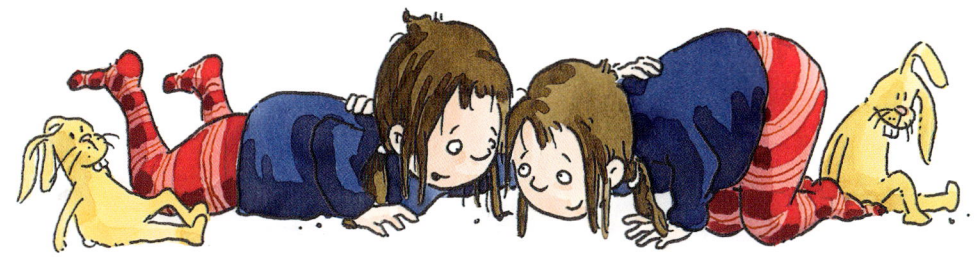

twins

sister

aunt

uncle

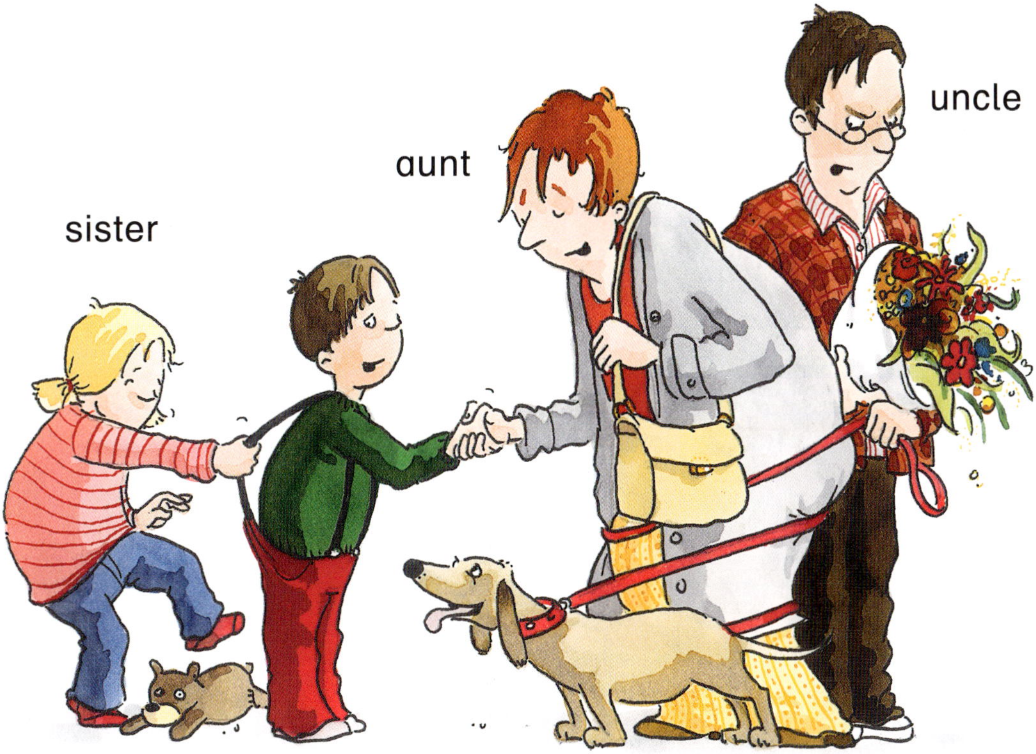

brother

First phrases

17 Do you like your 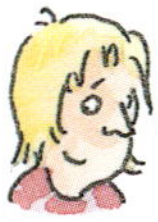?

Yes, I do. / No, I don't.

I don't have a 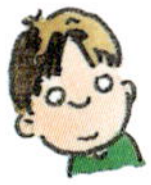.

Clothes

jacket

shoes

hat

watch

trousers

coat

dress

skirt

sunglasses

glasses

cap

shirt

sweater

shorts

boots

socks

19 I like wearing my  .

I don't like wearing my  .

At home

1 living room
2 kitchen
3 garden
4 bathroom
5 bedroom
6 door
7 toilet
8 stairway
9 window
10 hall

house

spoon

knife

glass

cup

bowl

plate

cupboard

fork

shower

soap

towel

bathtub

toilet

21

The 🥛 is in the kitchen.

The 🧻 is in the bathroom.

Furniture

table

fridge

bed

chair

shelf

wardrobe

curtain

coat rack

lamp

television

armchair

sofa

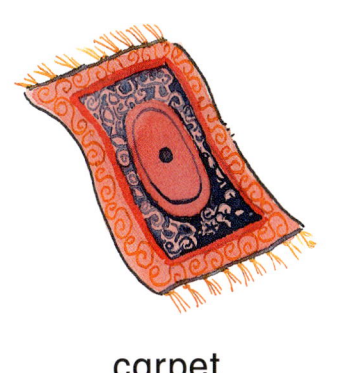

carpet

desk

23 Do you like this 🟨?

Yes, I do. / No, I don't.

Nature

spider

spider's web

fly

frog

flower

grass

meadow

bee

bird

bird's nest

stone

bush

river

lake

worm

ant

ladybird

tree

25 Can you see the ?

Yes, I can. / No, I can't.

Weather

sun

cloud

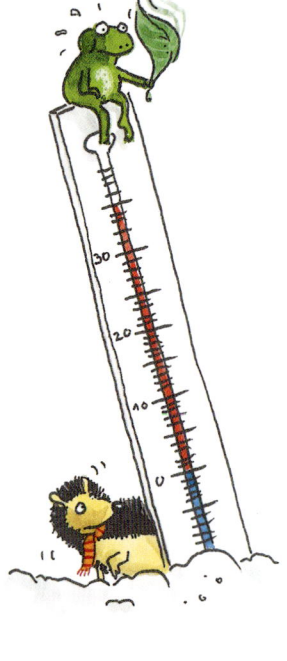

temperature

rainbow

rain

snow

lightning

thunderstorm

star

sky

fog

moon

wind

storm

27 How is the weather?

It is sunny. It is cloudy. It is rainy.

It is foggy. It is windy. It is stormy.

33

Vehicles

truck

taxi

sledge

fire engine

bus

train

helicopter

plane

car

motorbike

scooter

bike

ambulance

tram

I take the  .

Look at the  !

At school

book

pencil case

lunch box

glue

schoolbag

blackboard

watercolours

brush

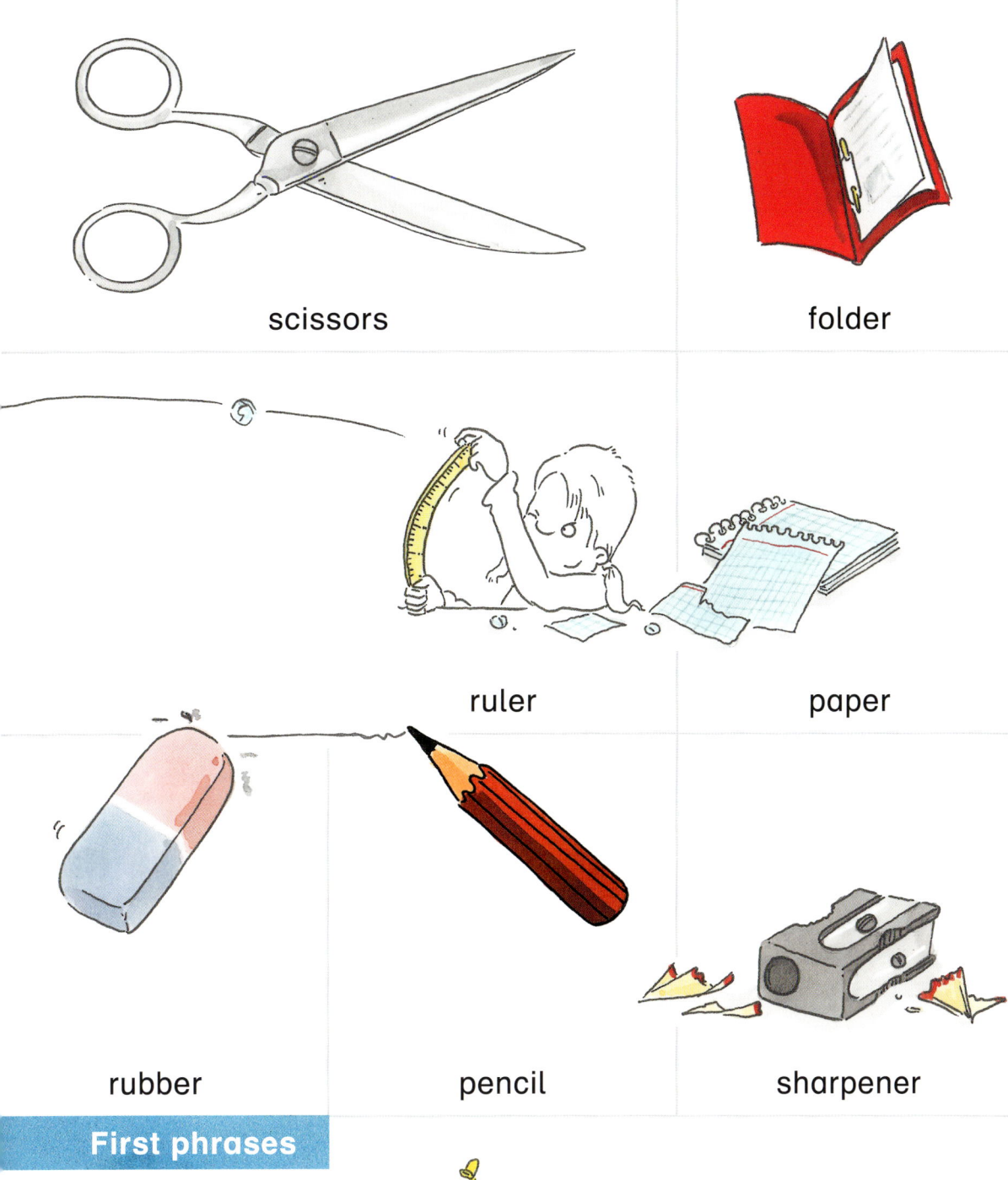

scissors

folder

ruler

paper

rubber

pencil

sharpener

31

Can I have the , please?

Yes, you can. / No, you can't.

Colours and shapes

brown

white

pink

blue

purple

yellow

red

orange

green

grey

black

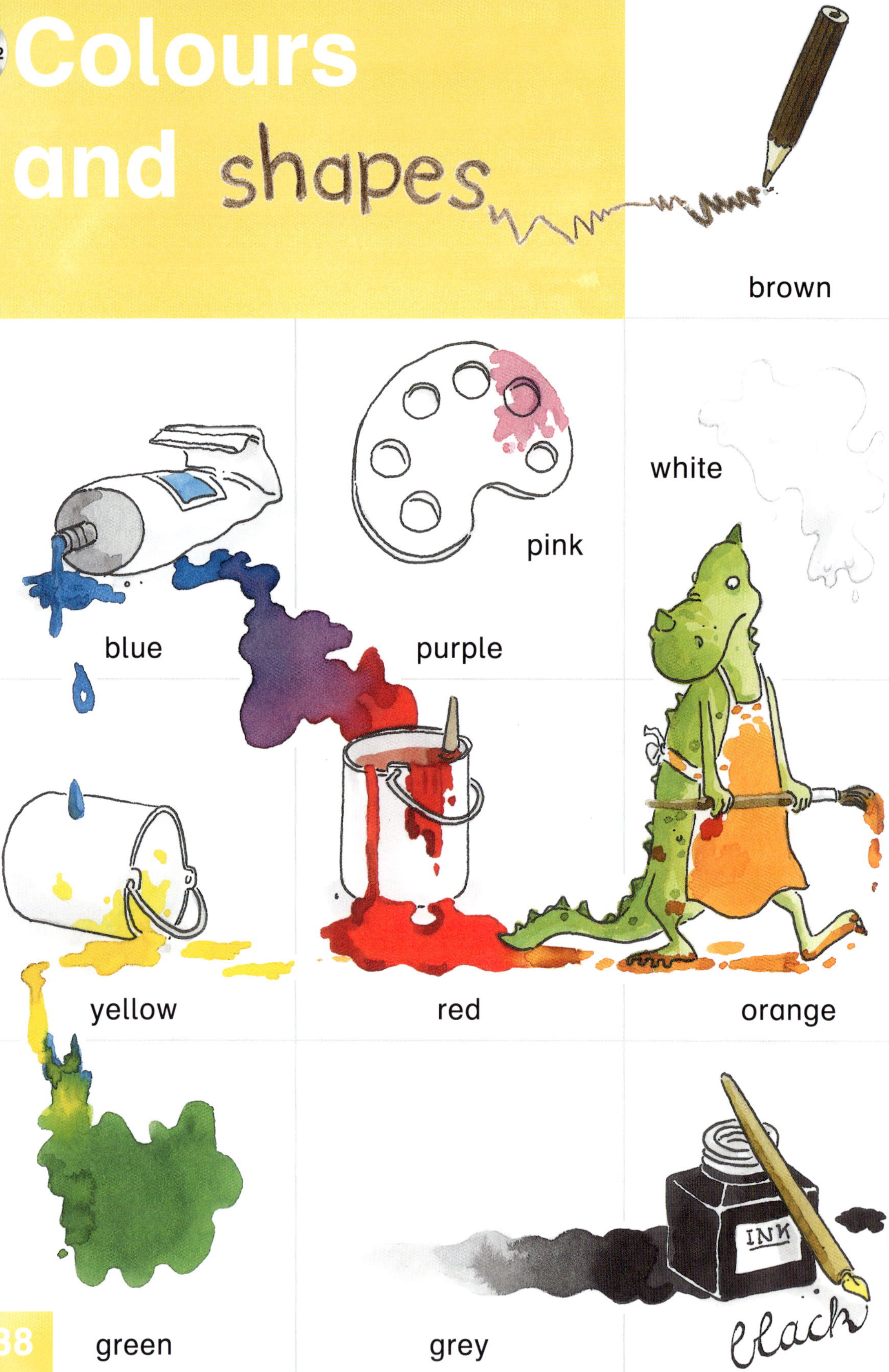

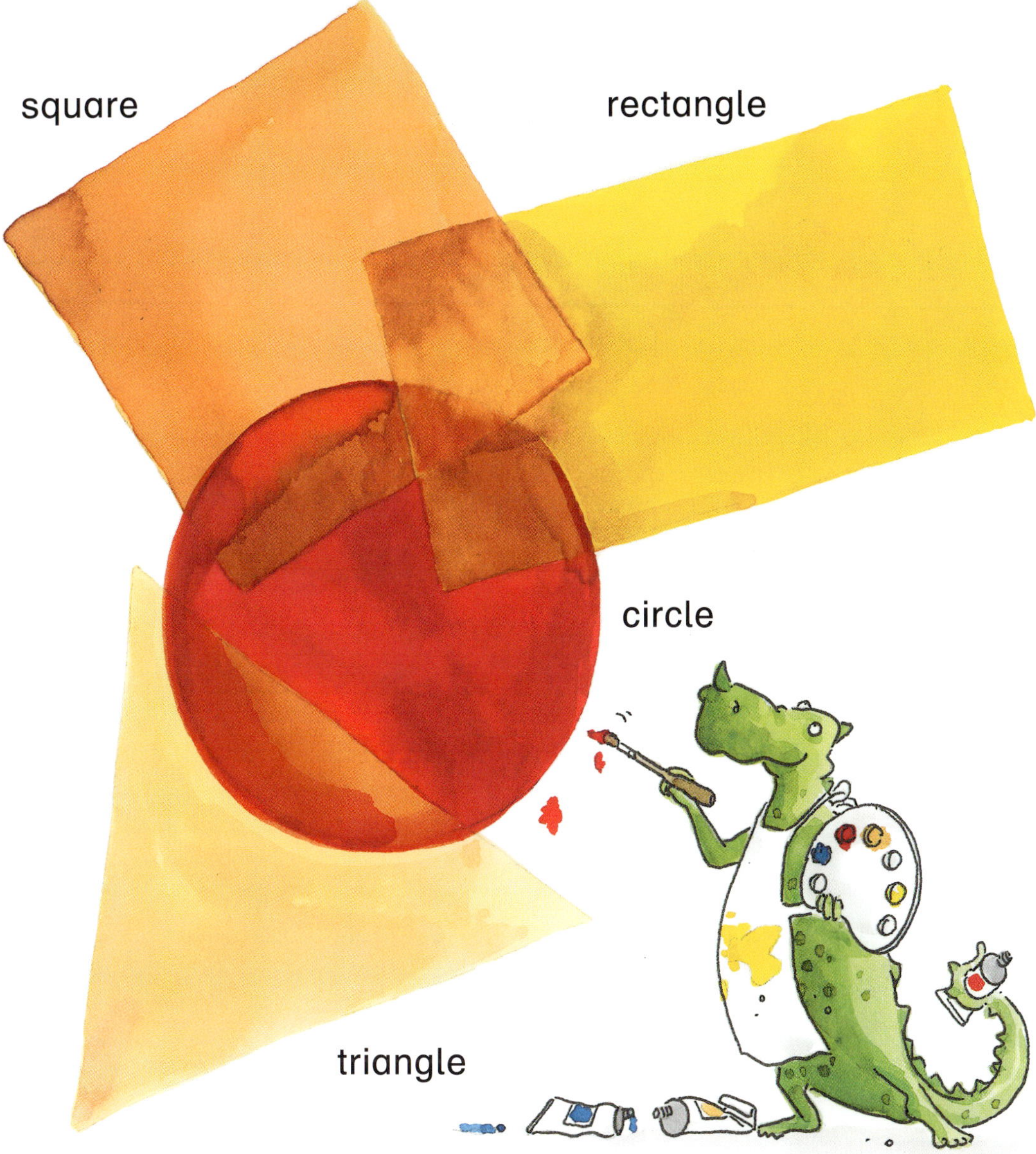
square
rectangle
circle
triangle

First phrases

33

The 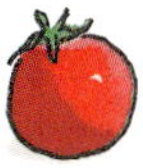 is 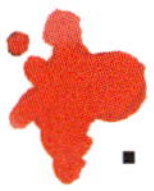.

The 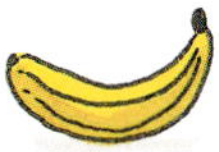 is 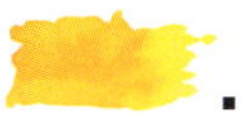.

Numbers

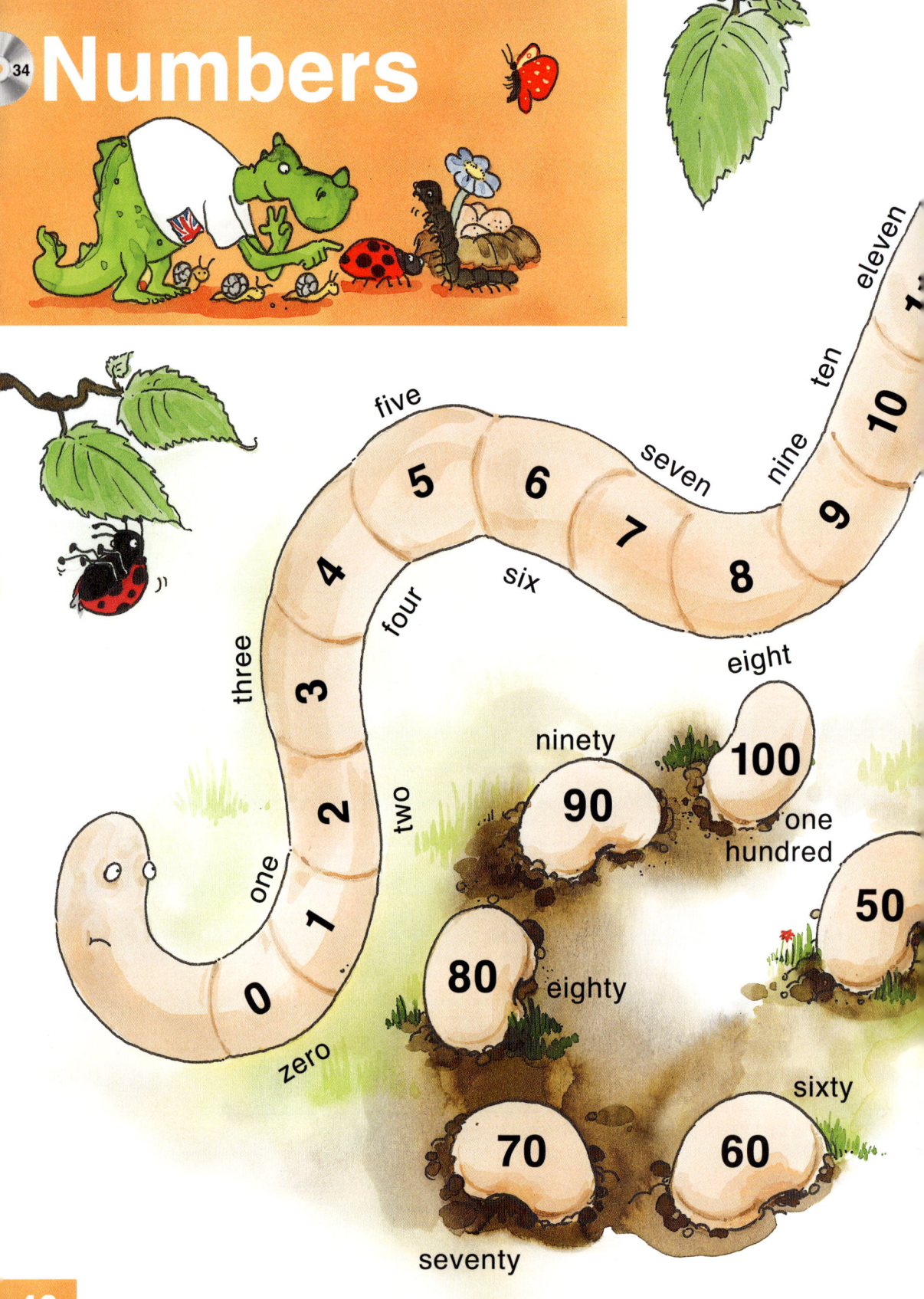

one
zero
two
three
four
five
six
seven
eight
nine
ten
eleven

0 1 2 3 4 5 6 7 8 9 10

ninety
eighty
seventy
sixty

100
90
80
70
60
50

one hundred

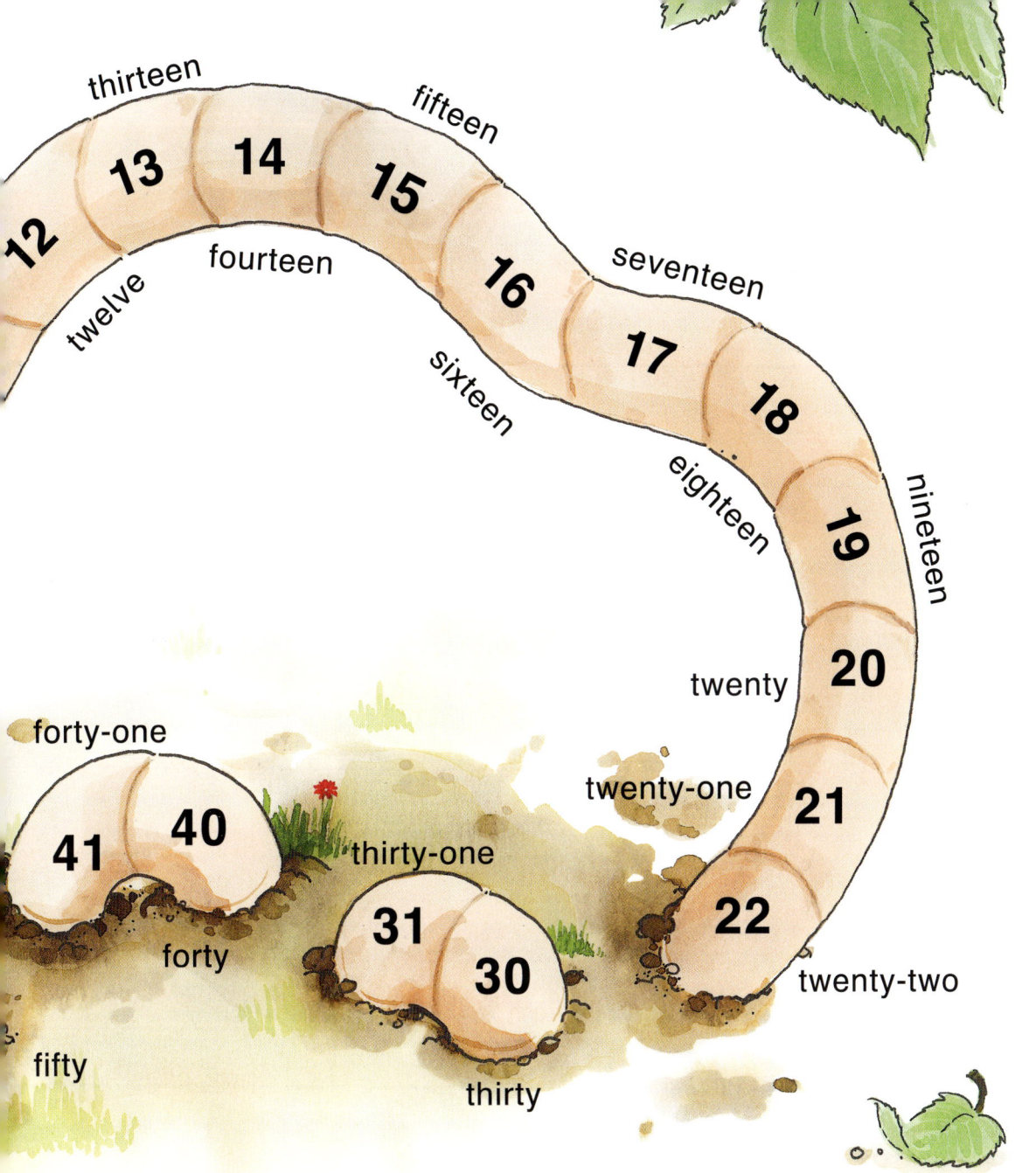

twelve
thirteen
fourteen
fifteen
sixteen
seventeen
eighteen
nineteen
twenty
twenty-one
twenty-two
thirty-one
thirty
forty-one
forty
fifty

First phrases

Please count from 4 to 12.

Please count from 11 to 5.

Calendar

Monday

Wednesday

Tuesday

Thursday

Friday

Saturday

Sunday

spring

summer

autumn

winter

37 What day is it today?

Today, it's Monday.

What month is it? It's July.

Opposites

left – right

quiet – loud

dry – wet

slow – fast

short – long

happy – sad

sweet – sour

thin – thick

dirty – clean

right – wrong

new – old

small – big

full – empty

good – bad

39 The opposite of 👦 is 👧.

Is the tree 🌳 or 🌳?

45

Jobs

mechanic

policeman

teacher

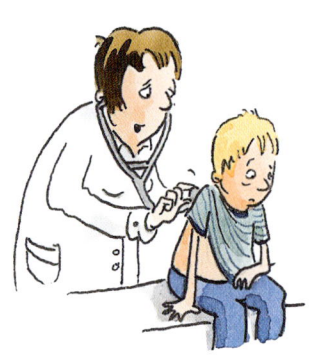

doctor

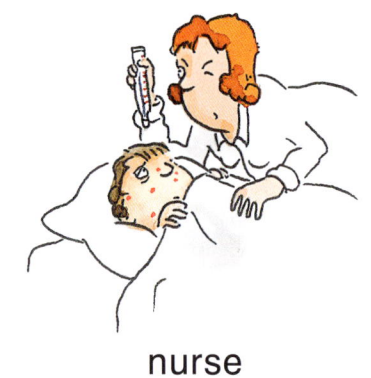

nurse

gardener

shoemaker

disc jockey

dentist

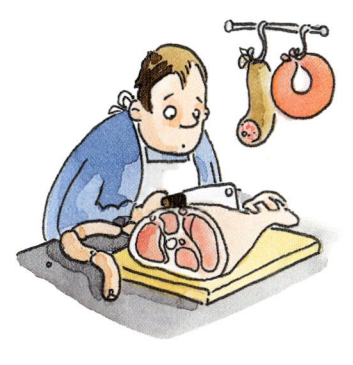

butcher

baker

cook

farmer   postwoman

hairdresser

fireman

41

Mrs Miller is a .

Mr Miller is a .

Special days

Christmas

Halloween

pumpkin

sweets

Santa Claus

biscuit

Christmas tree

birthday party

candle

present

cake

Easter

Easter egg   Easter bunny

New Year's Eve

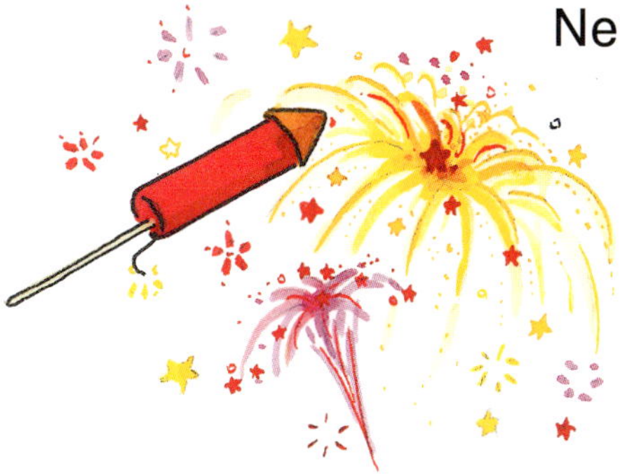

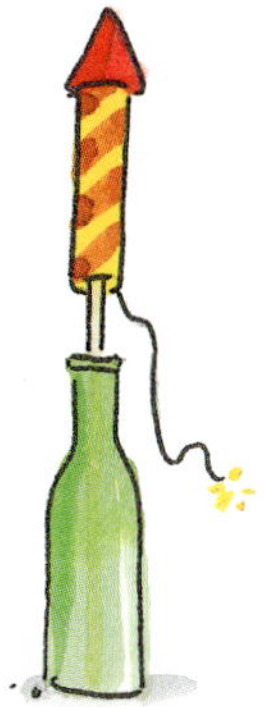

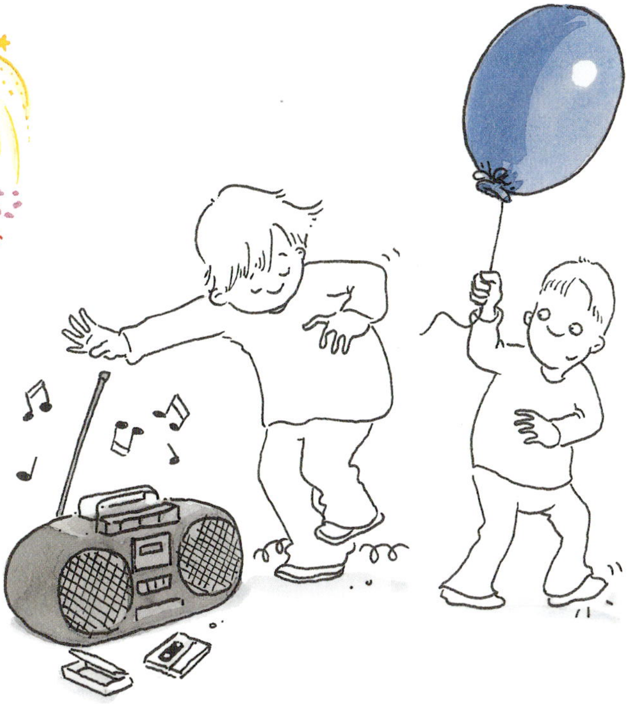

firework   music   balloon

43

Do you like Christmas?

Yes, I do. / No, I don't.

Do you like birthday parties?

First phrases (S. 8–27)

The monkey lives in the zoo.
The pig lives on the farm.

Where is the kitten?
Here it is.

Can I have the doll, please?
Here you are.
Yes, you can. / No, you can't.

Pass the bread, please.
Here it is.

Can I have a banana, please?
Can I have some cherries, please?
Yes, you can. / No, you can't.

I like eating lettuce.
I don't like eating cauliflower.

Show me your mouth!
This is my finger.

Do you like your mother?
Yes, I do. / No, I don't.
I don't have a brother.

I like wearing my dress.
I don't like wearing my hat.

The cup is in the kitchen.
The towel is in the bathroom.

Erste Sätze (S. 8–27)

Der Affe lebt im Zoo.
Das Schwein lebt auf dem Bauernhof.

Wo ist das Kätzchen?
Hier.

Kann ich bitte die Puppe haben?
Hier, bitte.
Ja. / Nein.

Gib mir bitte das Brot.
Hier, bitte.

Bekomme ich bitte eine Banane?
Bekomme ich bitte ein paar Kirschen?
Ja. / Nein.

Ich esse gerne Salat.
Ich mag keinen Blumenkohl.

Zeige mir deinen Mund!
Das ist mein Finger.

Magst du deine Mutter?
Ja. / Nein.
Ich habe keinen Bruder.

Ich ziehe gerne mein Kleid an.
Ich setze meinen Hut nicht gerne auf.

Die Tasse steht in der Küche.
Das Handtuch ist im Badezimmer.

First phrases (S. 28 – 49)

Do you like this table?
Yes, I do. / No, I don't.

Can you see the frog?
Yes, I can. / No, I can't.

How is the weather?
It is sunny. It is cloudy. It is rainy.
It is foggy. It is windy. It is stormy.

I take the bus.
Look at the fire engine!

Can I have the glue, please?
Yes, you can. / No, you can't.

The tomato is red.
The banana is yellow.

Please count from 4 to 12.
Please count from 11 to 5.

What day is it today?
Today, it's Monday.
What month is it?
It's July.

The opposite of happy is sad.
Is the tree thin or thick?

Mrs Miller is a nurse.
Mr Miller is a policeman.

Do you like Christmas?
Yes, I do. / No, I don't.
Do you like birthday parties?

Erste Sätze (S. 28–49)

Magst du diesen Tisch?
Ja. / Nein.

Siehst du den Frosch?
Ja. / Nein.

Wie ist das Wetter?
Es ist sonnig. Es ist bewölkt. Es ist regnerisch.
Es ist neblig. Es ist windig. Es ist stürmisch.

Ich fahre mit dem Bus.
Schau dir das Feuerwehrauto an!

Kann ich bitte den Klebstoff haben?
Ja. / Nein.

Die Tomate ist rot.
Die Banane ist gelb.

Bitte zähle von 4 bis 12.
Bitte zähle rückwärts von 11 bis 5.

Welcher Tag ist heute?
Heute ist Montag.
Welcher Monat ist es?
Es ist Juli.

Das Gegenteil von glücklich ist traurig.
Ist der Baum dünn oder dick?

Frau Miller ist Krankenpflegerin.
Herr Miller ist Polizist.

Magst du Weihnachten?
Ja. / Nein.
Magst du Geburtstagsfeiern?

Song

Good morning everybody,
oh, what a day!
It's warm and sunny weather,
let's go outside and play.

Skipping rope and my football,
puppets and my favourite doll,
don't forget the teddy bear,
let's take them all!

Melodie: Ein Männlein steht im Walde

Poem

A tomato fell asleep on a railroad track,
after a while it woke up.
The five-fifteen came rushing by.
Toot! Toot! Toot! Tomato ketchup!

Finger-play

Hello Mr Ticky Wick,
are you ready for a trick?
Can you see my little hands
with their tiny funny friends?
I can take them up and down
and can use them as a crown.

But the best thing I can do,
is – TICKLE YOU!

Counting-out rhyme

One, two, three,
please come with me.
Four, five, six, seven, eight,
let's go to the gate.
We missed the plane,
oh, what a shame.
Let's take the car!
Out you are.

1, 2, 3...

Playtime

Eating

I can set the table.

Do you like the soup?

Can I have some more, please?

Yummy, that's good!

Shopping

At school

On the way

At the restaurant

Saying goodbye

First phrases

Playtime (S. 56)

Come, play with me!
What do you want to play?
I want to play with the building bricks.
Okay, let's start.

Komm, spiel mit mir!
Was willst du spielen?
Ich möchte mit den Bauklötzen spielen.
Okay, fangen wir an.

Board games (S. 57)

Let's set up the game!
It's your turn.
Roll the dice.
I am the winner!

Lass uns das Spiel aufbauen!
Du bist dran.
Würfele.
Ich habe gewonnen!

Eating (S. 58)

I can set the table.
Do you like the soup?
Can I have some more, please?
Yummy, that's good!

Ich kann den Tisch decken.
Schmeckt dir die Suppe?
Kann ich bitte noch etwas bekommen?
Mmmmh, das ist lecker!

Shopping (S. 59)

I want to buy a puppet for my friend.

How much are they?
I'll take the witch.
Here is the money.

Ich möchte eine Handpuppe für meinen Freund / meine Freundin kaufen.
Was kosten sie?
Ich nehme die Hexe.
Hier ist das Geld.

At school (S. 60)

My name is Peter.	Ich heiße Peter.
What's your name?	Wie heißt du?
Can I sit next to you?	Darf ich neben dir sitzen?
Do you want to play with us?	Willst du mit uns spielen?
Let's meet this afternoon!	Treffen wir uns doch heute Nachmittag!

On the way (S. 61)

Where is the bus stop?	Wo ist die Bushaltestelle?
Go straight on!	Gehe geradeaus!
Turn left!	Gehe nach links!
Turn right!	Gehe nach rechts!

At the restaurant (S. 62)

Can I have the menu, please?	Kann ich bitte die Speisekarte haben?
I would like to have pizza with ham, please.	Ich möchte gerne Pizza mit Schinken.
Enjoy your meal!	Guten Appetit!

Saying goodbye (S. 63)

Goodbye!	Auf Wiedersehen!
It was nice to meet you.	Schön, dass ich euch/dich kennengelernt habe.
I hope to see you again.	Ich hoffe, euch/dich wieder-zusehen.

a b c d e f g h i j k l m n o p q r s t u v w x y z

ambulance 'æmbjʊləns	Krankenwagen	**A**
ant ænt	Ameise	
apple 'æpl	Apfel	
April 'eɪprəl	April	
arm ɑːm	Arm	
armchair ɑːmtʃeə	Sessel	
August 'ɔːgəst	August	
aunt ɑːnt	Tante	
autumn 'ɔːtəm	Herbst	

baby 'beɪbɪ	Baby	**B**
bad bæd	schlecht	
baker 'beɪkə	Bäcker/-in	
ball bɔːl	Ball	
balloon bə'luːn	Luftballon	
banana bə'nɑːnə	Banane	
bathroom bɑːθruːm	Badezimmer	
bathtub bɑːθtʌb	Badewanne	
beans biːnz	Bohnen	
bear beə	Bär	
bed bed	Bett	
bedroom bedruːm	Schlafzimmer	
bee biː	Biene	
big bɪg	groß	
bike baɪk	Fahrrad	
bird bɜːd	Vogel	
bird's nest bɜːdz nest	Vogelnest	
birthday party 'bɜːθdeɪ pɑːtɪ	Geburtstagsfeier	

67

biscuit bɪskɪt	Keks
black blæk	schwarz
blackboard ˈblækbɔːd	Tafel
blue bluː	blau
body ˈbɒdɪ	Körper
book bʊk	Buch
boots buːts	Stiefel
bowl bəʊl	Schüssel
bread bred	Brot
brother ˈbrʌðə	Bruder
brown braʊn	braun
brush brʌʃ	Pinsel
building bricks ˈbɪldɪŋ brɪks	Bauklötze
bus bʌs	Bus
bush bʊʃ	Busch
butcher ˈbʊtʃə	Metzger/-in
butter ˈbʌtə	Butter

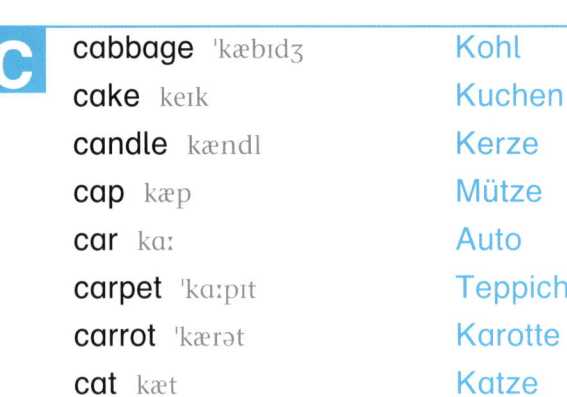

C

cabbage ˈkæbɪdʒ	Kohl
cake keɪk	Kuchen
candle kændl	Kerze
cap kæp	Mütze
car kɑː	Auto
carpet ˈkɑːpɪt	Teppich
carrot ˈkærət	Karotte
cat kæt	Katze
cauliflower ˈkɒlɪflaʊə	Blumenkohl
chair tʃeə	Stuhl

a b c d e f g h i j k l m n o p q r s t u v w x y z

68

cheese tʃiːz	Käse
cherries 'tʃerɪz	Kirschen
child tʃaɪld	Kind
children 'tʃɪldrən	Kinder
chin tʃɪn	Kinn
Christmas 'krɪsməs	Weihnachten
Christmas tree	Weihnachtsbaum
'krɪsməs triː	
circle 'sɜːkl	Kreis
clean kliːn	sauber
cloud klaʊd	Wolke
coat kəʊt	Mantel
coat rack 'kəʊt ræk	Garderobe
cook kʊk	Koch/Köchin
corn kɔːn	Mais
cow kaʊ	Kuh
cowboy 'kaʊbɔɪ	Cowboy
cucumber 'kjuːkʌmbə	Gurke
cup kʌp	Tasse
cupboard 'kʌbəd	(Küchen-)Schrank
curtain 'kɜːtən	Vorhang

D

daughter 'dɔːtə	Tochter
December dɪ'sembə	Dezember
dentist 'dentɪst	Zahnarzt/-ärztin
desk desk	Schreibtisch
dirty 'dɜːtɪ	schmutzig
disc jockey 'dɪsk dʒɔkɪ	Discjockey
doctor 'dɒktə	Arzt/Ärztin

dog	dɒg	Hund
doll	dɒl	Puppe
dolphin	ˈdɒlfɪn	Delfin
door	dɔː	Tür
dress	dres	Kleid
dry	draɪ	trocken
duck	dʌk	Ente

E

ear	ɪə	Ohr
Easter	ˈiːstə	Ostern
Easter bunny	ˈiːstə bʌnɪ	Osterhase
Easter egg	ˈiːstə eg	Osterei
egg	eg	Ei
elbow	ˈelbəʊ	Ellenbogen
elephant	ˈelɪfənt	Elefant
empty	ˈemptɪ	leer
eye	aɪ	Auge

F

face	feɪs	Gesicht
farmer	ˈfɑːmə	Landwirt/-in
fast	fɑːst	schnell
father	ˈfɑːðə	Vater
February	ˈfebrʊərɪ	Februar
finger	ˈfɪŋgə	Finger
fire engine	ˈfaɪə endʒɪn	Feuerwehrauto
fireman	ˈfaɪəmən	Feuerwehrmann
firework	ˈfaɪəwɜːk	Feuerwerk
flower	flaʊə	Blume

fly flaɪ	Fliege
fog fɒg	Nebel
folder ˈfəʊldə	Hefter
foot/feet fʊt/fiːt	Fuß/Füße
football ˈfʊtbɔːl	Fußball
fork fɔːk	Gabel
Friday ˈfraɪdeɪ	Freitag
fridge frɪdʒ	Kühlschrank
frog frɒg	Frosch
full fʊl	voll

G

garden gɑːdn	Garten
gardener ˈgɑːdnə	Gärtner/-in
ghost gəʊst	Gespenst/Geist
giraffe dʒɪˈrɑːf	Giraffe
glass glɑːs	Glas
glasses glɑːsɪz	Brille
glue gluː	Klebstoff
goat gəʊt	Ziege
goldfish ˈgəʊldfɪʃ	Goldfisch
good gʊd	gut
goose guːs	Gans
grandfather ˈgrænfɑːðə	Großvater
grandmother ˈgrænmʌðə	Großmutter
grandparents ˈgrænpeərənts	Großeltern
grapes greɪps	Weintrauben
grass grɑːs	Gras

green griːn	grün	
grey greɪ	grau	
guinea pig ˈgɪnɪ pɪg	Meerschweinchen	

H

hair heə	Haar
hairdresser ˈheədresə	Friseur/-in
hall hɔːl	Flur
Halloween hæləʊˈiːn	Halloween
ham hæm	Schinken
hamster ˈhæmstə	Hamster
hand hænd	Hand
happy ˈhæpɪ	glücklich
hard hɑːd	hart
hat hæt	Hut
head hed	Kopf
helicopter ˈhelɪkɒptə	Hubschrauber
hen hen	Huhn/Henne
honey ˈhʌnɪ	Honig
horse hɔːs	Pferd
hot chocolate hɒt ˈtʃɒklət	heiße Schokolade
house haʊs	Haus

J

jacket ˈdʒækɪt	Jacke
jam dʒæm	Marmelade
January ˈdʒænjʊərɪ	Januar
jigsaw puzzle ˈdʒɪgsɔː pʌzl	Puzzle
juice dʒuːs	Saft

July dʒʊˈlaɪ	Juli	
June dʒuːn	Juni	

king kɪŋ	König	**K**
kitchen ˈkɪtʃɪn	Küche	
kite kaɪt	Drachen	
kitten kɪtn	Kätzchen	
kiwi fruit ˈkiːwiː fruːt	Kiwi	
knee niː	Knie	
knife naɪf	Messer	

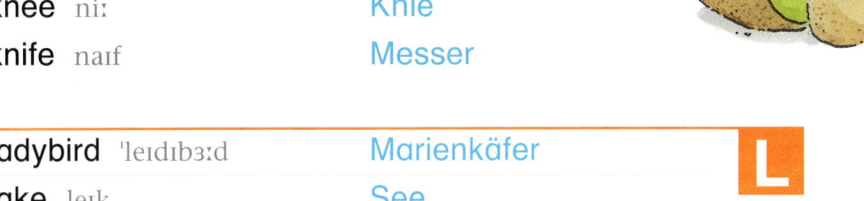

ladybird ˈleɪdɪbɜːd	Marienkäfer	**L**
lake leɪk	See	
lamp læmp	Lampe	
left left	links	
leg leg	Bein	
lemon ˈlemən	Zitrone	
lemonade leməˈneɪd	Limonade	
lettuce ˈletɪs	Salat	
lightning ˈlaɪtnɪŋ	Blitz	
lion ˈlaɪən	Löwe	
living room ˌlɪvɪŋ ruːm	Wohnzimmer	
long lɒŋ	lang	
loud laʊd	laut	
lunch box ˈlʌnʃ bɒks	Brotdose	

March mɑːtʃ	März	**M**
May meɪ	Mai	

meadow ˈmedəʊ		Wiese
mechanic mɪˈkænɪk		Mechaniker/-in
milk mɪlk		Milch
mineral water ˈmɪnərl wɔːtə		Mineralwasser
Monday ˈmʌndeɪ		Montag
monkey ˈmʌŋkɪ		Affe
moon muːn		Mond
mother ˈmʌðə		Mutter
motorbike ˈməʊtəbaɪk		Motorrad
mouse maʊs		Maus
mouth maʊθ		Mund
mushroom ˈmʌʃruːm		Pilz
music ˈmjuːzɪk		Musik

N

neck nek	Hals
new njuː	neu
New Year's Eve njuː jɪəz iːv	Silvester
nose nəʊz	Nase
November nəˈvembə	November
nurse nɜːs	Krankenpfleger/-in

O

October ɒkˈtəʊbə	Oktober
old əʊld	alt
onion ˈʌnjən	Zwiebel
orange ˈɒrɪndʒ	Orange/orange

paper	'peɪpə	Papier
parents	'peərənts	Eltern
parrot	'pærət	Papagei
peach	piːtʃ	Pfirsich
pear	peə	Birne
peas	piːz	Erbsen
pen	pen	Füller
pencil	'pensɪl	Bleistift
pencil case	'pensɪl keɪs	Federmäppchen
penguin	'peŋgwɪn	Pinguin
pepper	'pepə	Pfeffer
pig	pɪg	Schwein
pineapple	'paɪnæpl	Ananas
pink	pɪŋk	pink/rosa
plane	pleɪn	Flugzeug
plate	pleɪt	Teller
play dough	'pleɪ dəʊ	Knete
plum	plʌm	Pflaume
policeman	pə'liːsmən	Polizist
postwoman	'pəʊstwʊmən	Postbotin
potato	pə'teɪtəʊ	Kartoffel
present	'prezənt	Geschenk
princess	'prɪnses	Prinzessin
pumpkin	'pʌmpkɪn	Kürbis
puppet	'pʌpɪt	Finger-/Handpuppe
puppy	'pʌpɪ	Welpe
purple	'pɜːpl	violett

quiet	'kwaɪət	leise

R

rabbit	'ræbɪt	Kaninchen
radish	'rædɪʃ	Radieschen/Rettich
rain	reɪn	Regen
rainbow	'reɪnbəʊ	Regenbogen
rectangle	'rektæŋgl	Rechteck
red	red	rot
red pepper	red 'pepə	roter Paprika
right	raɪt	rechts/richtig
river	'rɪvə	Fluss
rubber	'rʌbə	Radiergummi
ruler	'ruːlə	Lineal

S

sad	sæd	traurig
salt	sɔːlt	Salz
Santa Claus	'sæntə klɔːz	Weihnachtsmann
Saturday	'sætədeɪ	Samstag
sausage	'sɔsɪdʒ	Wurst
schoolbag	skuːlbæg	Schulranzen
scissors	'sɪzəz	Schere
scooter	'skuːtə	Motorroller
September	sep'tembə	September
sharpener	'ʃɑːpnə	Bleistiftspitzer
sheep	ʃiːp	Schaf
shelf	ʃelf	Bord/Regal
shirt	ʃɜːt	Hemd
shoemaker	'ʃuːmeɪkə	Schuhmacher/-in
shoes	ʃuːz	Schuhe
short	ʃɔːt	kurz
shorts	ʃɔːts	Shorts

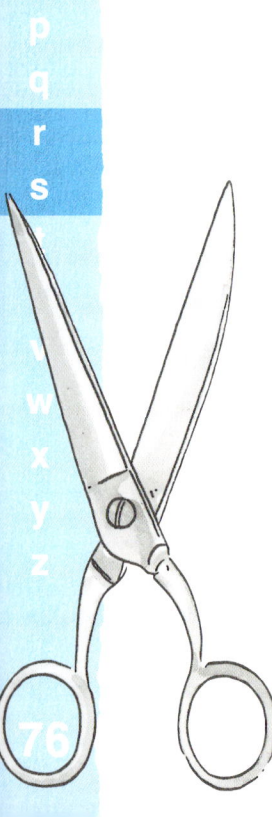

shoulder ˈʃəʊldə	Schulter	
shower ˈʃaʊə	Dusche	
sister ˈsɪstə	Schwester	
skipping rope ˈskɪpɪŋ rəʊp	Springseil	
skirt skɜːt	Rock	
sky skaɪ	Himmel	
sledge sledʒ	Schlitten	
slow sləʊ	langsam	
small smɔːl	klein	
snow snəʊ	Schnee	
soap səʊp	Seife	
socks sɒks	Socken	
sofa ˈsəʊfə	Sofa	
son sʌn	Sohn	
sour ˈsaʊə	sauer	
spider ˈspaɪdə	Spinne	
spider's web ˈspaɪdəz web	Spinnennetz	
spoon spuːn	Löffel	
spring sprɪŋ	Frühling	
square skweə	Quadrat	
stairway ˈsteəweɪ	Treppe	
star stɑː	Stern	
stone stəʊn	Stein	
storm stɔːm	Sturm	
strawberries ˈstrɔːbərɪz	Erdbeeren	
sugar ˈʃʊgə	Zucker	
summer ˈsʌmə	Sommer	

sun	sʌn	Sonne
Sunday	'sʌndeɪ	Sonntag
sunglasses	'sʌnglɑːsɪz	Sonnenbrille
sweater	'swetə	Pullover
sweet	swiːt	süß
sweets	swiːts	Süßigkeiten

T table	'teɪbl	Tisch
taxi	'tæksɪ	Taxi
tea	tiː	Tee
teacher	'tiːtʃə	Lehrer/-in
teddy bear	'tedɪ beə	Teddybär
television	telɪ'vɪʒn	Fernseher
temperature	'temprɪtʃə	Temperatur
thick	θɪk	dick
thin	θɪn	dünn
thumb	θʌm	Daumen
thunderstorm		Gewitter
'θʌndəstɔːm		
Thursday	'θɜːzdeɪ	Donnerstag
tiger	'taɪgə	Tiger
toe	təʊ	Zehe
toilet	'tɔɪlɪt	Toilette/Gäste-WC
tomato	tə'mɑːtəʊ	Tomate
tongue	tʌŋ	Zunge
tooth/teeth	tuːθ/tiːθ	Zahn/Zähne
towel	'taʊəl	Handtuch
toy car	'tɔɪ kɑː	Spielzeugauto
train	treɪn	Zug

train set 'treɪn set	Spielzeugeisenbahn	
tram træm	Straßenbahn	
tree triː	Baum	
triangle 'traɪæŋgl	Dreieck	
trousers 'traʊzəz	Hose	
truck trʌk	Lastwagen	
Tuesday 'tjuːzdeɪ	Dienstag	
turtle tɜːtl	Schildkröte	
twins twɪnz	Zwillinge	

uncle ʌŋkl	Onkel	**U**

wardrobe 'wɔːdrəʊb	Kleiderschrank	**W**
watch wɒtʃ	Uhr	
watercolours 'wɔːtəkʌləz	Wasserfarben	
watermelon 'wɔːtəmelən	Wassermelone	
Wednesday 'wenzdeɪ	Mittwoch	
wet wet	nass	
white waɪt	weiß	
wind wɪnd	Wind	
window 'wɪndəʊ	Fenster	
winter 'wɪntə	Winter	
witch wɪtʃ	Hexe	
worm wɜːm	Wurm	
wrong rɒŋ	falsch	

yellow 'jeləʊ	gelb	**Y**

Lautschrifttabelle

ɑː	wie in warm	arm
e	wie in Fleck	egg
iː	wie in Wiese	knee
i	wie in Baby	puppy
ɪ	wie in Tisch	pig
ɒ	wie in Frosch	frog
ʊ	wie in Hund	foot
uː	wie in Blume	room
ə	wie in Mutter	mother
aɪ	wie in Kleid	bike
aʊ	wie in blau	cow
ɔɪ	wie in neu	toy
ɪə	wie in Tier	ear
eə	wie in Meer	hair
ŋ	wie in Ballon	long
s	wie in Skelett	sofa
z	wie in Salat	zoo
ʃ	wie in Schule	shirt
tʃ	wie in tschüs	child
dʒ	wie in Dschungel	juice
v	wie in Vampir	van
æ	fast wie in Bär	bat
ɔ	fast wie in Horn	doll
ʌ	fast wie in Stadt	puppet
ɜ	fast wie in stört	bird

ei	*Diese Laute gibt es nur im Englischen.*	Monday
əʊ		pony
r		rabbit
ʒ		television
θ		tooth
ð		father
w		watermelon
b	*wie im Deutschen*	banana
d		doll
f		fish
g		garden
h		hand
j		yellow
k		cap
l		lemon
m		milk
n		nose
p		pink
t		taxi

Ideale Begleiter für die Kindergarten- und Vorschulzeit!

Nachschlagen, malen, rätseln, üben – mit diesen Büchern von Duden lernen Kinder ab 4 Jahren das Alphabet und die Zahlen. So gelingt der Schulstart sicher!

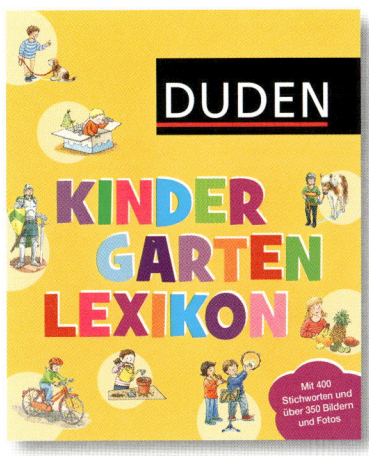

Das Abc
Mein Mitmachbuch
ISBN 978-3-7373-3239-2

Kindergartenlexikon
Mit 400 Stichwörtern und über 350 Bildern und Fotos
ISBN 978-3-7373-3043-5

Das große Vorschulbuch
Schreiben, Zahlen, Konzentration, Lesen
ISBN 978-3-7373-3036-7

Mein Kindergarten-Wortschatz
Sprachkompetenz optimal fördern
ISBN 978-3-7373-3202-6

Colours and shapes

Pets

Toys

At home

Numbers

Nature

Weather

Family

Clothes

Calendar

At school